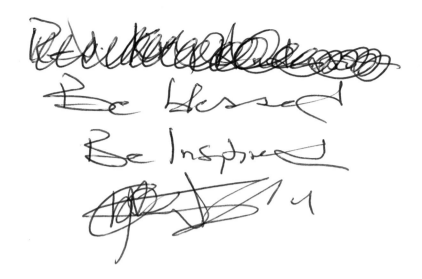

Be blessed
Be Inspired

Nuggets From The Night: An Anthology of Poetic Expressions

Vol. One

George Walters-Sleyon, PhD

This Book was printed in the United States of America.

The first edition published in 2020

ISBN: 9798364050243   Hardback
ASIN: B08QDSQH3C

To order additional copies of this Book, contact:

www.Amazon.com

Website: www.georgewalterssleyon.com

Introduction

Nuggets from the Night is an anthology of poetic expressions of over 200 poems written over the period of fifteen years. This anthology represents a mixture of social, meditative, political, theological, and existential expressions captured in poetic verses. They also aim to provide solace in the current climate of COVID-19.

Our individuality is grounded in the acknowledgment of our limitations. These limitations reflect our inadequacies on the way to self-discovery. The transition is not always self-generated, if we will admit it. Yet who we are, it seems, cannot exceed what we are attracted to or what attracts others to us. They are the attractions that do not necessarily imply negativity but interests influenced by the conditions of being a human: anxieties, loneliness, inadequacies, love, sickness, death, limitations in self-expression, the longing for fulfillment, the lack thereof, and the quest for significance. It has nothing to do with wealth, intellect, race, religion, tribe, and privilege. It has everything to do with who we are as human beings.

Yet the total expression of who we are lingers in the realm of natural and unnatural. Existence in the intersection between material and in-material describes our destiny. The adequate grasping of such in-between reality and the limitations in expressing it confound humanity, like the depth of the Sun.

Conflicted by social constraints, we are also conflicted by personal opinions. Out of the furnace of such conflicts, a new birth emerges that lives on the plain of self-awareness. Yet we reflect the tapestry of highlights and lowlights, sometimes leading us to the verge of extinction. It is this conundrum that we straddle through in our existence.

Expressions evade us, and language deceives us. Words are just the droplets of conflicted experiences silencing the volume of unspoken experiences. I wish to explore the depth of these implicit experiences as religious, social, political, and existential. They are experiences influenced by the duality of being profane and sacred, spiritual and secular, enfold in being human.

Table of Contents

Introduction 4

Dedication 12

The Existential

Soliloquy: The Complex Me 14

    The Divided Me 15

    Resistance 16

    The Dialectical Me 17

    What is Me? 19

    A Stranger unto Myself 21

    My Experiences I am 22

    The Scars of Existence 24

    The Lone Wave 25

    Not Born with the Golden Spoon 26

    Brought to a City 27

The Conflict of Job 28

    Job 12 29

    I Went to See the Judge Again 31

    What Shall I do? 33

    Waiting in Silence 35

    My Life is Eclipsed 37

    My Date with Destiny 39

Waiting I Wait 41

Job 10: My Complaint 43

I Must Find My Own Judge 44

The Solemn Anguish 45

The Flickering of Light 46

The Place of Security 48

In the Journey 50

Time Elapses 51

The End I Ponder 52

Directions Received 54

It Is Time 56

I Am Told to Go 57

The Attraction of the Unknown 58

The Thought of Freedom 60

Do This 62

The Night is Nearly Over 64

The Craving of the Soul 65

Signs to the Assigned 67

Love and Romance 69

Finding Love 70

Love is Distant 72

I Long for Love 73

The Departure of Love 74

For the Sake of Love 75

Love I Cannot Fake 76

For This Love I Wait 77

Come unto Me O Love 78

I am Made for Love 79

Sacred Love 80

The Aroma of Love 81

My Mother 82

Will it be? (July 22, 2010) 83

My Mother: An Enigma 85

I've Got No Mother? 87

The Living Dead 88

They Are Not Dead...89

Consult Not the Dead 90

The Reality

Society and Me 93

Society and Its Apathy..94

The Colorization of People 95

The Rationalization of Lies! 96

Fela Kuti Calls it the Democratization of Lies............................97

The Racialization of Crime! 98

The Colorization of Crime...99

The Racialization of Incarceration 100

The Colorization of Incarceration 101

They Refuse to See! 102

The Racial Conundrum 103

The Dripping of the Mystique 104

A Panegyric 106

Their Introduction to Civilization 107

The Religious Justification 108

Licensed by the Enlightenment 110

From Europe to Africa, Their Military Subjugation 112

From Africa to Europe: The Middle Passage 114

Africans on the Auction Block in Europe 116

The Heterosexual Slave Master 117

The Homosexual Slave Master 120

Abolition in Britain and America 121

Lynching! 122

Their Penal Subjugation 125

They Have Sinned Against God and the Africans 127

The World 130

The Ridiculous is Anointed! 131

The Ridiculous is Uncrucified! 133

The Heart is Cold! 136

The Confidence of the Soul 138

Can a Man Declare Himself Innocent? 139

The Pursuit of Ideas 140

The Threesome of Knowing 142

The Trouble of the Insecure 143

The Introspective

Cleansing.. 147

    The Process 148

    Turn Upon Yourself and Be Found!.................................149

    Limitation 150

    Beauty and Wisdom...151

    Above and Below in Contrast 152

    My Ten Principles of Life 153

Reflective Serenade.. 155

    The Piercing of Light 156

    I am Instructed..157

    Light Hidden in Darkness 159

    The Movement 161

    Know This..162

    The Struggle of the Soul 163

    He Sits in Solitude 165

    Drop the Gun!..167

    Nature and Notions 168

    Allow..170

    Learn the Ways of the Gentle Breeze 171

    Don't Be a Fool!...173

    Language Reflects my Limitation 175

    I am Down to My Last..177

    My Search for a Platform...178

Meditations 179

    Prayers I Will Offer! 180

    Help Me! 182

    This Twoness of Me 183

    O Lord Our Teacher! 184

    Where is God? 185

    Take Your Issues to the Lord in Prayer 186

    The Lord is My Shadow! 188

    What Do I Long For? 189

    God Has Not Brought Me This Far. 191

    When Your Niche Arrives! 192

    It is Not Late 196

Dedication

To the doctors, the nurses, the religious leaders, the scientists, the praying agents, the storekeepers, the retail workers, the garbage collectors, the street cleaners, the post office workers, the bus drivers, the grocery store workers and owners, the train drivers, the philanthropists, the pilots, the airport workers, the activists for social justice and respect for human dignity, the newscasters, the school teachers, the fathers, the mothers, the musicians, the comedians, the caretakers, the genuine politicians, and the unknowns working around the clock to help us survive the burden and angst of COVID-19. Thank you! May you find encouragement from these words and meditations.

The Existential

Soliloquy: The Complex Me

The human being is an embodiment of many complexities. Each individual always seeks an understanding of self-concerning others and what negates self. Following are the poems of self-reflection exploring the quest for self-understanding.

The Divided Me

I am a divided self.
This divided self I cannot maintain,
Undividedness, I do not know.
To dividedness, it seems I am bestowed,
Since my divided self is from within.

Must I not confess this divided me?
The search to end the battle within,
Battles not of internal will,
Battles not of external will,
Yet, to quell this division to Oneness I am directed.

George Walters-Sleyon

Resistance

O drag me not to the edge of this vault,
Draw me not to enter this veil.
Throw me not to the entry of this venom,
For I dread the enclave of this vice.

Fighting I fight to resist this projection,
Fighting, I fight to resent this pronouncement.
Fighting I fight to rebuke this presentment,
Fighting, I fight to reject this propaganda of me.

The prognosis is a deformation,
The prolepsis is a depreciation,
The diagnosis is a distortion,
Yet, the prescription I seek is Divine.

O drag me not to the edge of this vault
Draw me not to enter this veil,
Throw me not to the entrance of this venom,
For I dread the enclave of this vice

George Walters-Sleyon

The Dialectical Me

I am this
And not that.
I am that
And not this.

     I am that
     And not what.
     I am what
     And not that.

I am what
And not these.
I am these
And not what.

     I am these
     And not those.
     I am those
     And not these.

I am them
And not they.
I am they
And not them.

     I am they
     And not it
     I am it
     And not they.

I am what I am.
I am not what I am not.
I am that I am.
I am not that I am not.

George Walters-Sleyon

What is Me?

Knowing
I do not know.

Seeking
I do not seek.

Hearing
I do not hear.

When I know
I know, not what I know.

When I see
I see, not what I see.

When I hear
I hear, not what I hear.

To see
Is to see not.

To hear
Is to hear not.

To know
Is to know not.

O, what is me?
I know not.

I see not what is me
For I hear not what is me.

George Walters-Sleyon

A Stranger unto Myself

I am a stranger,
A stranger unto myself.
Little do I know about myself,
Only to stagger upon me.

The depth of me eludes me,
The interior of me is a subtle reflection.
To grasp me, I must gaze within
As the exterior of me is always fading.

George Walters-Sleyon

My Experiences I am

My experiences I am,
My experiences I reflect.
My experiences I deflect,
My experiences I select.
Since my experiences, I define.

A voice heard,
An event remembered,
A place visited,
A face recalled,
An encounter unforgotten.

They are experiences influenced,
They are experiences caused.
They are experiences designed,
They are experiences informed.
Yet experiences I embody.

I cherish the pleasant,
The unpleasant I defend not.
I cherish the remarkable,
The unremarkable I support not.
In divine solace, my experiences I seek to subdue.

Despise me not for my experiences; I am,
They are the scars I bear from my experiences.
Deny me not for my experiences; I am,
Flames of remembrance I often define,
For in human form, my experiences I am,

My experiences I am,
My experiences I reflect.
My experiences I deflect,
My experiences I select.
Since my experiences, I define.

George Walters-Sleyon

The Scars of Existence

Scars from yesterday have become scars of today.
The scars of the past want to define the scars of the future.
Scars of the night manifest in the day with definitions,
The scars of the day must not become the scars of the future.

The scars of the soul are scars from existence,
They are scars of scarcity that scare me.
I am scarred from the scars of existing,
Strength within is called upon to withstand these scars.

The scars that I speak of are not keloid,
Keloids are scars of mortal wounds.
The scars that I speak of are immortal wounds,
Keloids are transient scars with scientific tools.

The scars of the soul pursue the intervention of divine care,
It is care that does not scare me.
I am scarred from the scarcity of immortal care,
Providential care I seek to withstand the scars of existence.

George Walters-Sleyon

The Lone Wave

A Lone wave I have become!
The One to whom I disclose what I bear
Is the One with whom I dwell in peace.
The One to whom I display what I fear
Is the One with whom I dwell in pain.

I cannot mourn this identity,
It seems there is nothing I can now do.
I have done all I can in my power to do,
The tides still roll, but with caution, I hear.

The One to whom I disclose what I bear
Is the One with whom I dwell in peace.
The One to whom I display what I fear
Is the One with whom I dwell in pain.

The burden I bear I can share with no one,
Its intricacies I know with none to bear.
My tears I dry in consoling tones,
To face tomorrow with courageous songs.

George Walters-Sleyon

Not Born with the Golden Spoon

Your lot a pauper's throne,
Can you land a plenteous throng?

Not born with the golden spoon,
The silver lining is not your spoil.

The bronze was not given to you,
While the gold is a distance from you.

The struggle continues to achieve the dream,
But the height to define your choice it is.

Through the cultivation of seedling throngs,
To reap the seed enthroned.

Need abounds, and plagues do preach,
But the golden spoon is within your reach.

George Walters-Sleyon

Brought to a City

I wander about the plains of cities
Until I came to one.
I knew this was the One
It seems to be a home

George Walters-Sleyon

The Conflict of Job

This category of poems contains a mirror-like depiction of Job's experiences. In poetic forms, the Biblical figure describes and analogizes his life crises. He loses his seven children, wealth, wife, and dignity as a man of standing in his community. In these poems, Job's anxieties are captured like those of any other person.

Job 12

Laugh me not to scorn,
In the hands of Providence, I linger.
Mock me not to taunt,
In the arms of Providence, I sit

About this ordeal, I know but not the "other,"
Ask me for details.
I answer not in detail,
Details, I know, but in details, I cannot convey.

Mock me not, I plead,
Scorn me not, I pray,
Scold me not, I plead,
Mimic me not, I pray.

False, I am not,
Quasi, I am not.
Fictitious, I am not,
Phony, I am not.

The pseudo I am, I display in ignorance,
The fictitious I am, I display in illusions.
The phony I am, I display in delusions,
The quasi I am, in mockery I display,

Mock me not, I plead,
Scorn me not, I pray.
Scold me not, I plead,
Mimic me not, I pray.

George Walters-Sleyon

I Went to See the Judge Again

I went to see the judge again,
Not being discouraged is the strength of my soul.
Lingering in despair, my soul is afflicted,
Desiring to overcome, my soul is impacted.

Buffeted on many sides, the trials I endure,
Struck by hopes dashed to pieces.
My soul in anguish longs to overcome,
The endurance of pain to its abode of peace.

From the chaos of anarchy, my dreams survive,
To attain the height of the solemn peak.
Though bleak my path may be, this hope I dare not relinquish,
My cherished dreams I received to survive.

The odds may come, but the oath still stands,
A vision of the light my soul has seen.
In the crucible of darkness, this light is conceived,
The odds to defeat and the oath to receive.

I will not throw away my cherished dreams,
When troubles come to test my plans.
My dreams have become my noble flames,
I will abound in ceaseless streams.

I look within for the soothing voice,
Assuring me of approaching bliss.
If, in your trials, you withstand this vice
In droves of fulfillment, you will be blessed!

George Walters-Sleyon

What Shall I do?

I am caught on the plains,
The plains of no growth.
I am caught on a plan,
A plane of no grounding.
What shall I do?

The gate is locked,
The doors are clocked,
The curtains are drawn,
The keys are dispensed with.
Where shall I go?

The fountain is dry,
The funds are down,
The wells are empty,
The walls are erased.
What shall I do?

The phone rings no more,
The doorbell sounds no more,
The dog barks no more,
The knob turns no more.
Where shall I go?

I am caught in a place,
A place of no grain.
I am hooked on a platform,
A platform of no graduation.
Where shall I go?

George Walters-Sleyon

Waiting in Silence

In silence, I wait,
In silence, I fret not,
Fretting, I despise.
In silence, I am felt,
Felt in what I do,
Doing what leads to silence.

How long must I wait?
While hope diminishes,
Feeling like a lost boat.
Floating on the sea of despair,
With a feeling of drifting,
Only desiring to be anchored.

I cannot tell it all.
In the telling, I am not understood.
In silence, I am misunderstood.
In actions, I am misinterpreted.
I search to know,
But knowing eludes me.

I long to enter in,
But only a glimpse, I see.
I long to embrace it,
But only a glimmer I grasp.
I long to encounter it,
But only its glamour, I see.

When will it be?
How long will it take?
How long must I wait?
Repeated longing
In silence, I wait,
For in silence, I shall overcome.

Waiting is patience
In silence, I must endure
In silence, I must endeavor
In silence, I am ensured
Waiting is empowerment
Since in silence, I encounter

George Walters-Sleyon

My Life is Eclipsed

My life is eclipsed
I must bear the waiting.
No further can I move
My movement is watched.

My life is eclipsed
This fate, I must bear.
In patient endurance,
My longing is fulfilled.

To pursue is to perceive
To perceive is to participate.
To participate is to attend,
To attend is to apprehend.

The choice I have is derailed,
The desire I seek is unknown.
Inescapable plans I know prevail,
Until the choice for me is known.

My life is eclipsed
Until then, my lot I bear.
Yet, this treasure I dare to possess,
While the passing of age, I must fear.

Misunderstood, in silence I stand,
Misconceived, from a distance, I speak.
Misinterpreted, in solitude, I walk,

Misperceived, from the surreal, I resign.

My life is eclipsed.

George Walters-Sleyon

My Date with Destiny

I wake up in the morning
I am reminded of this ordeal.
To think about the end
Is to forget about mourning.
The tightening of issues around me
Is more than the ideal.
My hope alone is hope within
Hope that abounds beyond my pain.

To share it with others
Is to think of the impossibility.
Will the hope I share come to pass?
Will it be shattered to no repair?
I marvel at the faces
To see marks of implausibility.
Left with much despair
I take solace in the hope of being.

In this place, it is handed to me
Of darkness, I genuinely remember.
Told it would require of me a costly price
I am reminded to intercede for its fulfillment.
A gift was given in somber reflection
Its price I must not despise.
Only to request strength to stand
I am bowed in social contrition.

Against the odds, the price produces,
A date with destiny, it seems I simply have.

To cancel this date, I am inclined to resist,
In its fulfillment, I must persist.
I cannot return to my previous date,
Its promises I doubt to quench my thirst.
My date with destiny is a confident hope,
Since its premise is divinely certain.

George Walters-Sleyon

Waiting I Wait

Waiting, I wait.
How long I know not,
Longing for appearance.
Longing not for the disappearance,
Waiting, I wait.

How long I know not,
Hoping for arrival,
Hoping not for the absence.
Waiting and waiting is the fate I bear,
Waiting to perceive is the burden I bear.
While time elapses in silent fear,
I ponder my future with severe tears.

Waiting, I wait.
How long I know not,
Wanting to touch.
Wanting to be touched,
Waiting, I wait.

How long I know not,
Waiting, I have waited,
Waiting, I thwart not.
Others, I perceive, have acquired their lot,
Awaiting my lot, I dream only in nightly rest.
Waiting, I see only in nightly zest,
Yet my peace I receive from the timeless Lord.

Waiting, I wait.
How long must I wait?

I do not know.
In silence, I wait
Silence is arriving, and waiting is remaining.

George Walters-Sleyon

Job 10: My Complaint

I must complain because I wish to know,
Yet to know I cannot grasp.
Eluding me, I gasp to know,
To know I desire, to understand I seek.

I know; therefore, I complain,
Suffer me not the complaint of ignorance.
For in ignorance, I am not complaining,
Since, in ignorance, I seek not to know.

I complain to understand!
The fullness of this ordeal I desire to know.
What I know I know not in the fullness,
Fleeing from me is the certainty of knowing.

I will complain to comprehend this ordeal,
In seeking to know, I seek to understand.
This I know, to be apprehended
To grasp this experience in knowledge, I will pursue.

George Walters-Sleyon

I Must Find My Own Judge

I must find my own judge,
A judge who respects my dignity.
A judge who rescues me from this bondage of indignity,
I must find my own judge.

George Walters-Sleyon

The Solemn Anguish

Peace I request in this time of trial,
The contentment I request in this moment of adversity.
Rest I desire in this time of wandering,
Solemnity I want in this moment of despair.

Secured in the place of rest,
Freed from the traps of conflicting assaults,
Saved in the shadows of assurance pouring,
I Am secured in this place of rest.

A beggar I have become to survive this test,
While my closest friends laugh me to scorn.
I must lean on the solace that revives,
With this confidence, this too shall pass

I shall not perish, I tell myself,
In this ordeal, I know I am safe.
When in anguish, my soul is raised
In perfect alignment, my body is led.

George Walters-Sleyon

The Flickering of Light

With the flickering of light am beginning to see,
Always believing in believing the impossible.
The test of courage to withstand,
Under the weight of uncertainty, I had fallen.

Knowing that the end will prove inevitable,
The burden of the angst is real.
Always challenged by the need to arrive,
The lifting of my heart to expected harmony.

Time trickles by in absolute stillness,
Thinking this stillness is waiting for me.
Time does not give up at my door,
Yet in gradual achievement, this passing I know.

From a distance, the pressure abounds,
Reminding me of my commitment to stand.
When will this burden be lifted, I wonder?
In gentle remover, I sense a movement.

Informed by a song that deliverance is near,
I look to see its flickering appearance.
Its arrival I have longed for so long,
Conceived within me is the reality of peace.

Waiting is no longer the position, I assume,
Receiving is the position I retain in the process.

The reality I craved has passed before my eyes,
In concrete reality, it's arrival I receive.

George Walters-Sleyon

The Place of Security

To retreat from this stormy fog,
I must return to my sacred refuge.
This refuge I know I cannot refuse,
Its security, I know is the orphan's home.

In the bliss of Love, the anguish falls,
To the rising snares of agony to avoid
I cherish the solace of its spring. I am available,
Its price to bear with my soul I afford.

I cannot doubt no not its surety,
To bask in its assurance, I have resolved.
Time and tears my lot; it seems,
I have this hope all angst will dissolve.

My goals within I shall attain,
Goals to obtain I did not seek.
Their origin of the surreal beginning,
To accompany their aim, I am retained.

A trend I seek to maintain this quest,
The both of us a request surreal
To fill the needs of the prevailing request
I shall return with surreal assurance.

I cannot deny the reality I bear,
The fact of unrelenting appearance I see.
To me, this reality in music heard,
Yet, with the naked eye, its activities are unseen.

To the place of security, I will return,
It's abiding peace the insecure cannot steal.
It is the place where my struggle ceases,
To return to the world with strength renewed.

George Walters-Sleyon

In the Journey

These poems seek to capture the human expectation to achieve a goal, arrive at a relished destination, or attain the expectations of a treasured vision. However, all these probabilities are frothed with uncertainties, challenges, and other oddities that seek to make human longing profoundly impossible. On the other hand, victory and the prospects to arrive can occur if we keep pressing on.

Time Elapses

Time evades me; I am not eclipsed.
I stand in its embrace,
Wrapped in its confidence.
Rejecting its collapse,
In its shadow, I stand.

Time escapes me
As I bask in its evasion.
Marked by its desertion,
In the mirror, I gaze,
Only to gasp at its design in departing.

Time elapses,
Yet hope is refreshed.
This hope of flooding rays,
This light of enormous radiance,
To bask in the shadow of timeless hope.

Time eludes me,
But I am standing,
I refuse to give up.
Time has mocked me,
But I carry on in the sphere of timelessness.

George Walters-Sleyon

The End I Ponder

I ponder the end of this journey.
What will become of me?
How will this story end?
I want to know,
I made some mistakes,
But I did what I was told to do.

I knew I was led to do something,
The conviction was my overwhelming strength.
Moved by truth, I plunged in,
I leaped into the unknown.
The leap was not one of ignorance,
My conviction about the unknown was real.

The consequences of my action I must endure.
Even good intentions will sometimes be uncertain.
But will this good intention go bad? I ponder,
Longing for a change, my eyes I raise to the hills.
In anxiety, I call upon the One who knows me best,
With peace unexpected, my soul is flooded.

Was I wrong to begin this journey?
Was I wrong to have responded to this call?
Was I wrong to have said yes to what I heard?
Spare me the scorn,
Understand my plight,
I, too, ponder the end as I consider my fate.

Will I be the victim of my decision, I wonder?
Will I bear the brunt of mockery?
To endure the pointing of fingers,
To survive the turning of faces at the entrance of my shadow.
Who decides and does not lament the outcome?
Who makes decisions and does not ponder the end?

But I hear the consoling whisper
—Your cause I will vindicate,
On this path, I have led you.
The justice of your cause will I vindicate,
Little did you know that you were led."
With this consolation, I ponder in peace.

George Walters-Sleyon

Directions Received

1. Guidance from a distance comes,
Instructions from beyond appear,
Caution from behind, I hear,
Warning from the yonder prevails.

2. Sometimes a fool, I think to trust,
To relinquish my reliance, I fear.
In silence, the inquiry of guilt condoned,
This "coming to me," I ponder.

3. To go away, it cannot decide,
To me, it seems attached forever.
Why should this attachment persist,
When my abode is a failing tent?

4. Inquiries I constantly make,
Investigations I pursue daily.
To another who is aware of this phantom, I inquire,
To find a companion of life experiences.

5. You are alone in your castle, I hear.
To another, a different burden to bear,
Each on a path of destined faith,
To shake it off rebellion abounds.

6. On another, the spark may fall,
   On another, the spark is placed,
   On another, the spark is forced,
   To shine like stars in unbridled style.

7. Instructions I received to walk this path,
   Guidance comes to walk this distance.
   Caution I hear to walk in this knowledge,
   Warning prevails to order my path.

8. What if it does not happen? I inquire,
   A question I ponder every day.
   The past I have to refer to daily,
   The present I know to define the future

George Walters-Sleyon

It Is Time

It is time to go, linger not,
It is time to be gone, linger not.
It is time to leave, linger not,
It is time to cleave, linger not.

Notice the unsolicited counsel,
Notice un-petitioned assistance.
Notice the un-demanded company,
Notice the un-requested voice.

Wait no more to depart,
Wait no more for departure.
Wait no more in the department,
Wait no more in your apartment.

The inkling to leave has arrived,
The inkling to leave abounds.
The inkling to leave from above,
The inkling to leave has appeared.

It is time to go, linger not,
It is time to be gone, linger not.
It is time to leave, linger not,
It is time to cleave, linger not.

George Walters-Sleyon

I Am Told to Go

This morning I was told to go,
This week I am reminded to go.
This morning I am reminded to go,
In the night, I am encouraged to go.

My left leg reminds me it is time,
My right leg informs me it is time.
My thoughts remind me it is time,
While the events remain with me in time.

Wondering where to go,
Searching for where to go.
Seeking a place where to go,
Pondering on where to go.

It appears while cleaning the kitchen,
It appears while I am cooking.
It appears while sitting in solace,
It appears when taking a nap.

To know it is time to go is absent,
To know it is time to go to is present.
To know it is time to go is preferred,
To know it is time to go, I am aware.

George Walters-Sleyon

The Attraction of the Unknown

I am attracted to the unknown,
Its unknown beauty is appealing.
The necessity to trust the unknown is refreshing,
In the process of trusting, I must relinquish,
For relinquishing is the condition for trusting.

Confounded by the inclination to the unknown,
I am assured to trust.
The assurance to trust the unknown is consuming,
The dissipation of fear I am conscious of.
The unflinching assurance to be cared for is sure.

This certainty of the unknown I acknowledge,
Not informed by outward security.
Inward awareness springs up, and certainty speaks of safety,
The known I am confronted with,
But to the unknown, I am attracted.

Caught in the attraction of the unknown,
Drawn to the influences of its orchestrations.
Difficult the grasping yet possible the growing declares,
Trusting in the unknown is the sailing from the known,
I am caught in the embrace of the unknown.

To be led by the unknown, I am confident,
To be wedded to the unknown, I am secured.
To be sworn to the unknown, I am assured,

To be attracted to the unknown, I am aware,
For in the unknown, I linger.

George Walters-Sleyon

The Thought of Freedom

The trap was set,
But I was brought out.
Trapped in its claws,
I was wiggled out,
Only to be set on a muddy path.

What do I do?
I've got nowhere to go.
Whom do I call? I do not know.
My anxieties I share,
Only to be snared at.

To be vulnerable, I dread.
To be naked, I fear,
Naked once, I was crushed.
Vulnerable once I was trashed,
A laughingstock I was left to be.

My situation I am aware of,
My helpers I was told to be aware of.
What will the end become?
I ponder daily,
A fool I refrain from becoming again.

Did I make the wrong choice?
Have I made the right choice to believe?
A believer I have become,
The pain of believing I do express,
The peace of believing I always request.

The victory I desire comes from afar,
The visit I desire to set me on fire.
It is the coming from a distance.
The constant coming with persistence,
Simply to appear with promises spoken.

George Walters-Sleyon

Do This

Do this,
In doing this
You will come to that.

Listen to this,
In listening to this
You will incline.

Depart from here,
In departing from you here
You will arrive there.

Resist not the wind of departure,
For departing
You shall arrive.

Depart not in ignorance,
For ignorance is remaining
Departure is arriving.

Be wary of them that respect not.
They speak with haughtiness
For that is all they know.

They enter with arrogance,
The world is their footstool
But they lack substance.

Wealth they have,
Worth they lack,
Influence they purchase.

Know the boisterous from afar,
Escape with your heart
For your heart defines your life.

Know the ignorant from afar,
Escape with your head
For your head decides your thoughts.

Know the virtuous from afar,
Embrace virtue yourself
For virtue will reduce your vices.

Do this
In doing this
You shall arrive.

George Walters-Sleyon

The Night is Nearly Over

The night is nearly over
The dawn is almost broken,
The moon is almost covered
The sky is nearly wakened.

Behold the mourning receding,
Behold the morning proceeding.
Behold the mocking regressing,
Behold the morrow progressing.

Reject the past its demeaning,
Renounce the past and its demerits.
Remind the past of its meaning,
Restore the past and its merits.

The night is nearly over,
The dawn is almost broken.
The moon is almost covered,
The sky is nearly wakened.

George Walters-Sleyon

The Craving of the Soul

The craving of the soul is a word of guidance,
It orchestrates the soul into the path of Providence.
Provided to disprove the fear of failing,
Provided to approve the fate of excelling,
But against the odds of constant failure.

The craving of the soul is a word of instruction,
Flowing from the depth of the human foundation.
Given in the moment of human reflection,
Given in the moment of human selection,
A word in conflict with human defections.

The craving of the soul is a word of assurance,
A Word from beyond human existence.
Spoken in the crevices of deep despair,
Spoken from the cradle of the Divine,
A word at odd with sudden destruction.

The craving of the soul is a word of fulfillment.
Bringing in its wings the hope of attainment.
Bestowed in the season of constant interruption,
Bestowed for the reason of careful intervention,
A word in tension with open insurrections.

Some things are given,
Some things are inherited,

Some things are acquired,
Some things are attained.

Yet the craving of the soul is gently bestowed.

George Walters-Sleyon

Signs to the Assigned

Signs are to the assigned!
When no sign is seen, it is a sign,
A sign is a sign when there is no sign.
Signs to the assigned do not require signs,
Since the assigned signs are present.

To interpret a sign is to see a sign,
Signs to the assigned precede signs.
To interpret a sign is to know a sign.
To know a sign is to see a sign,
Signs are known to those who know them.

To know a sign is to know a sign.
Not to know a sign is to know a sign,
Signs are known when there is no sign.
To despise a sign is to know a sign,
Signs appear to all as signs.

The fool knows a sign when there is no sign.
To see a sign is to know a sign,
The absence of a sign is the presence of a sign.
A sign present is a sign absent,
A sign absent is a sign present.

Search for a sign and see a sign.
Search for no sign and see a sign,
Signs appear when signs are needed.
Signs are not needed, and signs appear,
The source of a sign a sign does not know.

The source of a thing the thing does not know.
Signs appear since signs are sent,
Signs are sent to the assigned as signs.
To know a sign is to see a sign,
To see a sign is to know a sign.

To the assigned, a sign is known.
To know a sign is to understand a sign,
To understand a sign is to see a sign.
To see a sign is to know a sign,
The assigned knows a sign since they are assigned.

To the unassigned, the assigned is a sign.
The absence of a sign is the presence of a sign.
See a sign and know a sign,
Know a sign and see a sign,
Since to see a sign is to heed a sign.

Sitting at a counter, I saw an African woman. Beautifully dressed in matching African attire. She was talking to a man who said, "when there is no sign, there is no sign." But she responded, "when there is no sign, that is a sign." The fool looks for a sign he derives, but the sign he sees is the sign he despises. I agreed with her and was awakened to write (Recorded: 10-September-08).

George Walters-Sleyon

Love and Romance

The quest for Love is universal. When true Love is stumbled upon, the heart is lifted in ecstasy and fulfillment. Similarly, the spirit is restless until it finds true and fulfilling Love. Notwithstanding, the heart may never experience such Love and will have to make do with what it already has. But such a void of true Love can also be filled with only the taste of divine Love. These poems depict the quest for Love—Love of the Heart: romantic, existential, and spiritual.

Finding Love

Many girlfriends are not wives,
Many wives are not girlfriends.
Many men are not husbands,
Many husbands are not boyfriends.

The man who finds a wife in a friend is blessed,
A woman who finds a husband in a friend is blessed.
The man who finds a friend in a wife needs a wife,
A woman who finds a friend in a husband needs a husband.

Some marry for security,
Some marry for wealth.
Some marry for lust,
Some marry for friendship.

The man who finds a friend in a wife is blessed,
A woman who finds a friend in a husband is blessed.
The man who finds a wife in a friend needs a wife,
A woman who finds a husband in a friend needs a husband,

To marry for security is to be insecure,
To marry for wealth is to be poor.
To marry for lust is to be the lost,
To marry for friendship is to be alone.

Many girlfriends are not wives,
Many wives are not girlfriends.
Many men are not husbands,
Many husbands are not boyfriends.

George Walters-Sleyon

Love is Distant

I know how it feels,
I have felt it before.
Feeling so real,
An indication of Love.

It was Love that I felt,
Love that I long for.
Love so distant,
It was Love that I felt.

I search for Love,
In this One, I look.
In that One, I look,
The Love I cannot find.

Love has turned its back on me,
It has left me standing alone.
Love has turned its back on me,
It has left me for distance.

George Walters-Sleyon

I Long for Love

Love's return I long for,
Love's embrace I long for.
Love's gentle breeze I crave,
Love's soft breath I crave.

Despise me not,
Love has left me alone.
Despise me not,
Love is hidden from me.

Toward me, Love has closed her eyes,
To my whisper, Love has sealed her heart.
Towards me, Love has folded her arms,
To my sighing, Love has protected herself.

This longing for Love is real,
In the wilderness, I have wandered.
Awaiting the arrival of Love,
Love separates from the foggy mist of desire.

George Walters-Sleyon

The Departure of Love

Why this long?
Why this departure?
The answer I do not know,
Only with questions, I am familiar.

The wind blows my way sometimes,
And Love, I think, has arrived.
The door I open, but the dust of Love I see,
There I stand with eyes filled with tears.

Love's inward witness, I know,
Yet loves absence I am aware of.
Love's inner witness, I know,
Yet, of its absence, I am conscious.

Reason I apply to understand Love's departure,
I must discover the departure of Love.
Love I reflect upon to pursue,
Love I reflect upon to prevail

George Walters-Sleyon

For the Sake of Love

Self I deflect to encourage Love,
"I" I denounce to pursue Love.
"Me" I resist partaking of Love,
"Ego" I despise embracing Love.

For Love, I am separated,
The Love I once knew will not come.
Love stands aloof,
The Love I once knew refuses to come.

Of this freeing of my soul in Love, I am aware,
Of this freedom in my soul in Love, I am aware.
Of this rest in Love, I am conscious,
Since the lightness in my feet indicate Love.

In this Love that I crave,
My soul is ablaze.
In this Love that I crave,
My song is Love.

George Walters-Sleyon

Love I Cannot Fake

The faking of Love I desire not,
This pretense of loving I despise.
The deceit in Love I despise,
This faking of Love I desire not.

I cleanse for Love,
In the morning, I awake to see Love.
At night I am alone without Love,
Love is not false.

Must I create Love as I am told?
Must I purchase Love, as I often hear?
Must I fabricate Love as I see it done?
Must I declare Love when the heart is distant?

Despise me not O Love,
Be not far away, O Love.
Come unto me in time,
In time I crave your timeless embrace.

George Walters-Sleyon

For This Love I Wait

I will wait for Love,
I am bottled up with Love.
For Love, I am ready,
Its absence has prepared me.

When Love knocks on my door,
Love's signal, I will know.
The lack of Love has taught me,
Love's inklings, I know.

Tease me not for my desire for Love,
Scorn me not since I crave Love.
Without Love, I am aloof,
Without Love, I am lost.

I must wait for Love,
How long, I know not.
Only if Love could come soon,
My longing would be no more.

George Walters-Sleyon

Come unto Me O Love

Come to me, O Love,
And ease my silent sigh.
Come to me, O Love,
And cease my silent pain.

Love immeasurable,
Love unimaginable.
Love unfathomable,
In Love, I delight.

Beyond the façade of the senses,
Beyond the farce of the senses,
Informing the action of the senses,
Informing the acts of sensuality.

True love, the spring of the soul's freedom,
True love, the source of my song,
True love, the source of my delight,
True Love, the spring of my soul's desire.

Come unto me, O Love.

George Walters-Sleyon

I am Made for Love

In Love, I am made whole,
From the pieces of me,
In Love, I am healed,
The gathering of my parts.

In the fullness of Love, I am redeemed,
In the fullness of Love, I am restored.
In the fullness of Love, I am reconciled,
In the fullness of Love, I am reborn.

Cover me with Love,
For Love is my covering.
Heal me with Love,
Love is my healer.

In Love, I am enlightened,
This sighing for Love.
In Love, I delight,
For this Love, I am made.

George Walters-Sleyon

Sacred Love

I am falling in Love,
With caresses of ecstatic touch,
It is Love of the "Other,"
It is a touch of the "Other."

I am beckoned at the breaking of dawn,
to engage with Love.
It is Love that I find exhilarating,
Dripping on the edges of my back.

It is a touch I find exuberant,
Stripping off the edges of me.
I am conscious of this Love,
Perceptively alive in the abyss of my conscience.

Consciously radiant in the halls within,
Love of this nature, I know.
Love of this touch, I feel,
But the Love of this posture I see not.

George Walters-Sleyon

The Aroma of Love

This Love is like the sweet smell of hibiscus perfume,
This Love of morning mist in fragrant fumes,
This Love of evening dawn at setting Sun,
Has me aglow with tender blooms.

I have fallen in Love,
Unshackle, not this tender loom.
Dishevel not this delicate bloom,
I have fallen in Love.

It is Love not of perishing sight,
Search to uncover a precious scent.
It is the Love of enduring embrace,
It is the Love of eternal embrace.

I have fallen in Love,
To love not the figment of Love.
To live in Love, an unfathomable experience,
I have experienced Love, not the phantom of Love.

George Walters-Sleyon

My Mother

These poems capture the passing of one's mother/father, especially in one's absence. Have you lost your mother/father and were not there— in the hospital, at her home, or far away? You wish you were there, but circumstances made it impossible. It has been several years, months, weeks, or days since she departed this earth. Do you think you still have a mother, or do you not have a mother because she is dead?

Will it be? (July 22, 2010)

Concerns innumerable,
Anxieties inescapable,
I am at last at the end,
The end is insurmountable.

My mother, I long to see,
Her face I long to sealed again.
Her hands I desire to clasp,
The touch my soul knows.

Into her eyes, I desire to look,
To grasp the unbroken claims of Love.
The mother I saw several years ago,
The mother I desire to behold.

Her ailing heart, my absence increases,
My departure, first joyful, has turned mournful.
Her end I dread to often hear,
Her pain, I fear, may increase at will.

With every telephone call, I wonder,
The phone rings her departure. I dread.
To be kept in longing, I opt for,
With every ring from this number, my fear returned.

Will it be that our eyes should lock?
Will it be that our arms should clasp?
Will it be that I run to her embrace?
Will it be that I smile when she smiles?

How long will it be before my departure?
The departure to behold her face.
The face in years I haven't seen,
The presence in years I desire to enjoy.

George Walters-Sleyon

My Mother: An Enigma

Raised in solitude,
Embraced in the solitary.
A quest to satisfy,
A life too mystified.

A profound smile she carried always,
The laughter she spread around always.
A joke to soothe the increasing pain,
A joke to smoothen the fear around her.

Sacrifice she made for the passing stranger,
Her home she opened to the stranger in need.
A stranger she claimed we all are,
Strangers, she believed we are indeed.

My mother an enigma

Her encounter with God an absolute experience,
Central to her life was this divine encounter.
To trust in God was her absolute mission,
To the weary soul, her quest to proclaim.

Life without God is painful, she declared,
Humility she proclaimed as the highest virtue.
Know your weakness, she always said,
A life of pride is a stumbling block.

My mother an enigma. I know as such,
A beauty reflected in serene knowledge.

Not in material wealth, she always sparkled,
But in divine knowledge, she found her spark.

My mother an enigma.

George Walters-Sleyon

I've Got No Mother?

What I dreaded finally happened,
The call I feared rang so loud.
Trembling, I responded to its bidding,
This call I knew, and I have dreaded.

It finally came, and I was distraught.
Did I miss an opportunity to go?
Why am l left with this sense of loss?
Only to gaze at the setting Sun.

"I've got no mother," I declared in tears,
A motherless child I have become.
The succor of a mother,
I no longer have.

Yet, in a daze of dreaming, I became aware,
The face of my aunt I construed her to be.
Only to turn; it was my mother's face,
Consoling me with words I had declared.

"And yet you said, 'I've got no mother."

George Walters-Sleyon

The Living Dead

Are they dead, or are the dead living? Have you ever wondered if your deceased relatives are dead or if they are living? It is not living in some country in the world. But living.

They Are Not Dead

They are not dead,
They are alive.
Hidden from human eyes,
They speak continuously.

They have not gone,
They are present.
Hidden from sight,
They appear to the eyes.

The family lives on, I hear,
The family lives on, I see.
Therefore, be aware of the second eye,
The eye that sees you in constricted places.

When they depart to their own, they appear,
Something in Christ declares they are alive.
In Christ they died. In Christ they live,
To appear to their own from a distance near.

George Walters-Sleyon

Consult Not the Dead

The dead are alive,
The departed are present.
Returning to their very own,
To comfort their weary ones.

Yet, consult not the dead on behalf of the living,
From the land of the living, they have departed,
Call not the dead on behalf of the living,
From the land of eternity, they carry out orders.

At the bidding of the living, they do not come,
Instructions they receive but not from the living.
The living in the natural knows, not the dead.
The dead in the un-natural is familiar with the living,

Seek not the dead in the place of the living,
Some are restrained from appearing to the living.
Some are reserved to appear to the living,
However, with orders, are they dispatched to the living?

George Walters-Sleyon

The Reality

Society and Me

A society thrives on the stratification of its members. It is the right of the stratified to unyoke themselves for good or for bad. These poems seek to describe the angst for justice, fairness, equality, and respect for human dignity in poetic expressions.

Society and Its Apathy

The private sign is obvious solipsism,
The public sign is abject narcissism,
The prevailing sign is overt misanthropy.

Hopeless individualism is a cultural sign,
Rancorous secularism the societal sign,
While the flight of Love is the doom assigned.

Vindictive Love in the social fabric,
Vindictive penology is the penal psychic,
Vindictive apathy is a social psychosis.

Return to love your human Love,
Your pristine laws a deceptive love,
The coldness of your heart, your prisons love.

George Walters-Sleyon

The Colorization of People

White people!
Black people!
Yellow people!
Brown people!

The process of imposition,
The start of stigmatization,
The concept of conscription,
The making of marginalization.

Yellow eyes!
Brown eyes!
Green eyes!
Black eyes!

In the label, identity is concrete
In the label, ideas are confused.
In the label, humanity is dying.
In the label, humanity is dead.

George Walters-Sleyon

The Rationalization of Lies!

The White lies!
The Brown lies!
The Yellow lies!
The Black lies!

Lies in colorization,
Lies configured.
Lies concocted,
Lies in corroboration.

The racialization of lies.
The rationalization of lies.
The radicalization of lies.
The rascalization of lies.

George Walters-Sleyon

Fela Kuti Calls it the Democratization of Lies

The democratization of lies!
The demo-cracy-tization of lies!
The demonstration of crazy lies!
The crazy demonstration of lies!

Lies in politicization.
Lies in propertization.
Lies in professionalization.
Lies in prisonization.

The toleration of democratic lies,
The tolerance of demo-cracy-tization of lies.
The toleration of crazy democratization of lies,
The tolerance of crazy demonstrations of lies.

George Walters-Sleyon

The Racialization of Crime!

White crimes,
Brown crimes,
Yellow crimes,
Black crimes.

The racialization of crimes,
The racist notion of crimes.
The racial sentencing of crimes,
The racializing of crimes.

White crimes engender sympathy,
Yellow crimes engender empathy.
Brown crimes engender apathy,
Black crimes engender apartheid.

George Walters-Sleyon

The Colorization of Crime

Crimes in racial colorization,
Crimes in the color of the criminal.
Crimes in the color of race,
Crimes in the racialization of color.

The criminalization of race,
The racial criminalization of race.
The criminalizing of race,
The racial incrimination of race.

Crimes in racial profiling,
Crimes in the profiling of race.
Crimes in the profanation of race,
Crimes in racial profanation.

George Walters-Sleyon

The Racialization of Incarceration

White incarceration,
Brown incarceration,
Yellow incarceration,
Black incarceration.

The racialization of incarceration,
The racist incarceration of race.
The racistization of incarceration,
The racialization of incarcerating race.

George Walters-Sleyon

The Colorization of Incarceration

The colorization of incarceration,
The incarceration with color consciousness.
The colorizing incarceration of color,
The conscious incarceration of color.

Incarceration in color,
The coliseum of color incarceration.
Incarceration in the colorist conscience,
Yet, the colossal incarceration of Colored People.

George Walters-Sleyon

They Refuse to See!

Do they see the effects of their actions?
Do they feel the effects of their passion?
In unconscious patterns, they express a nature,
In conscious awareness, they fashion to torture.

Assuming a posture of indelible ink,
It is a reflection of the wealth acquired.
Consciously created as a social link,
Only in colors is this wealth reflected.

Consigned to inscrutable pain, the other is aware,
Caught in the crucible of the war of anxiety.
Prone to inquire into this belligerent action,
Only to be caught in the tirades of the oppressor.

George Walters-Sleyon

The Racial Conundrum

Subjected to scorn and apathy in the back,
Reduced to objects and projections in the front.
A thief and a robber they claim you are,
While the mirror not too far speaks otherwise.

Multitude they have reduced to things for use,
To enrich the masses at their pleasure and wimps.
Distorted to embrace a twisted nature,
Destroyed to reject the super-nature.

Intentionally designed to perpetuate this distortion,
To assert a lie when the truth is absolute.
God and Jesus, Allah and Muhammed, they strangely claim,
When in God and Jesus, Allah and Muhammed their deeds
we know!

George Walters-Sleyon

The Dripping of the Mystique

Drip, drip, drip,
The dripping of the mystique.
Drip as it drips,
Droplets of its mystique.

The uncovering of its magic,
The discovery of its misery.
Drip, drip, drip,
The dripping of the mystique.

Drips in rhythmic beats,
The tempo is challenging to hear.
Droplets at the beat of largo,
The slowness is negating adagio.

Pianissimo at its fineness,
Majesty in discord.
Drip, drip, drip,
The dripping of the mystique.

The dripping of the mystique,
Dripping, dripping, dripping.
Dripping in the presence of all,
All in the company of the mystique.

The mystique demystified,
For in dripping, de-mystification abounds.
The pace of dripping sounds,
The face of the mystique is uncovered.

Drip, drip, drip,
The dripping of the mystique.
The eyes behold it,
Held in the hands are droplets.

Droplets hands will not keep,
For in keeping, misery abounds.
Murder in misery abounds,
Since in the mystique, the hidden limps.

Drip, drip, drip,
The dripping of the mystique.
From security, it leaps to insecurity,
To be, it must despise.

To despise mystique must linger,
Slashing the security of those despised.
While it abounds in despising,
The mystique de-mystified.

The mystique de-mystified,
Droplets, drip, dripping.
Drip, drip, drip,
The fading of the façade.

The demise of illusion,
Drip, drip, drip.
The dripping of the mystique,
Drip, drip, drip.

George Walters-Sleyon

A Panegyric

The collection of poems in this category is designed to provide a narrative of the various stages of the transatlantic slave trade and their intellectual justification, religious justification, economic justification, and existential implications. In poetic descriptions, they capture the transatlantic slave trade and the institution of slavery in poetic expressions.

It is an oxymoron the conscience cannot bear,
That democracy will dabble in this abuse of humanity!
It is an oxymoron the conscience cannot bear.

Their Introduction to Civilization

To name a person is to define that person.
To name a people is to distinguish them as those people.
To stereotype a race is to degrade that race.
To name a continent is to systematize that continent.

The quest to define was the quest to limit.
The quest to distinguish was the quest to separate.
The quest to stereotype was the quest to dehumanize
The quest to systematize was the quest to stigmatize.

Enslavement and Colonization, the tools to define
To rule to the despair of the enslaved and the colonized.
The colonized, they thought, brought dignity.
Yet, dignity is bestowed with hidden disdain.

To civilize, they came in boats from afar.
The savage in need of civilization,
It was a civilizing process to curb their savage rage.
Yet, to the rage of the civilized, the savage fell!

George Walters-Sleyon

The Religious Justification

The sailing of ships to Africa to Islamize,
The sailing of ships to Africa to Christianize,
The sailing of ships to Arabicize
The sailing of ships to Westernize.

Gold and Ivory the Muslims sought.
In the depletion of their treasures,
Africans, their carriers, the Muslims sold.
To the West, Islam introduced its savage hosts.

In the Middle East, Africans they traded,
Perfect workers, the Arabs considered them to be.
Black pigmentation the Arabs saw beneath them,
But for economic reasons only of value.

Savage, they were in the Middle East.
Cheap labor to provide for their Islamic superiors.
For Islamization, Africans were perfect
Arabization in external reflection.

To Christianize the Africans, the Portuguese came.
They saw their hearts significantly transformed
Since the Africans are "notoriously religious."
But, to enslave them was their prudent choice.

To Christianize the absolute goal.
Christ the Messiah to bring to the weary.
But beneath the Holy Cross was the dungeon's way,
From Elmina Castle to the Middle Passage.

George Walters-Sleyon

Licensed by the Enlightenment

The Enlightenment is the root of Western intellectual racism!
Europeans, the race of supreme intelligence
White complexion, the superior race,
Black complexion, the inferior race.

Pseudoscientific theories they advanced,
The signs of inferiority they have discovered,
To justify the material distinctions,
Darker skin, they declared dissimilar.

For David Hume, the Sun is the cause of black pigmentation.
Emmanuel Kant boasted that blackness is a sign of stupidity
For Georg Hegel, the Germans are the superior race.
But Thomas Jefferson considered Sally Hemings below his
whiteness, yet his mistress with his six children.

Black inferiority, they declared, was anatomical.
Big lips and flattened nose,
Big penis and big buttocks,
With immense disdain for the African complexion the
Enlightenment pioneers established their names.

The oblong head is a sign of the smallest brain they wrote.
Indeed, they claimed the African's head a sign of inferiority.
The European's head a sign of a bigger brain and superiority
But indeed, the Black skin, they argued an absolute
Degeneration.

The Enlightenment Era provided intellectual vindication.
This racial genocide science also aided.
Monogenesis to polygenesis, the denigration of the Adamic
Race.
Yet, fake science is the foundation of racial superiority.

George Walters-Sleyon

It is an oxymoron the conscience cannot bear,
That democracy will dabble in this abuse of humanity!
It is an oxymoron the conscience cannot bear.

From Europe to Africa, Their Military Subjugation

Three Legs of Subjugation they embarked upon,
From Europe to Africa with military artilleries.
From Africa to the Americas with slaves and gold,
From the Americas to Europe with raw materials.

The Belgians were involved; ask the Congolese.
The Portuguese were involved, ask the Brazilians.
The British were involved, ask the Commonwealth of Nations.
The Spanish, the Scotts, and the French were fierce slave
masters; ask the Indians, the Jamaicans, and the
Algerians.

They came with guns, rum, and sugar.
They came with religion, greed, and racial superiority.
They left with gold, the young and the old their human
cargos.
The Continent of Africa, they came to pillage.

The sowing of internal conflicts was their strategic choice,
Divide and conquer among the chiefs the only means,
To threaten the local chiefs with invasion was very strategic,
The African bodies and raw materials their utmost choice.

Africans in nativity have seen the white man!
In the Ghanaian language, "a god" is seen.
Hospitality abounds to appease their gods,
Yet, with motives ungodly, their gods are consumed.

Africans on Africans was a sure recipe,
Tribes on tribes the perfect strategy,
While tribalism prevailed in the West and the East,
African tribalism is the worst, they claim,
Over 11 million they dragged through the Middle Passage!

George Walters-Sleyon

From Africa to Europe: The Middle Passage

The trade in human beings was their ultimate goal.
Elmina Castle and Sudan, the absolute reflection,
To enrich the West in the human trade,
While the East, its Arabization spread.

They pillaged the culture of their savage host!
The strongest from 10 to 40 were deliberately stolen!
Men and women to perpetuate the community,
They were placed on ships through the Middle Passage!
With slave-sticks on their necks, they hauled their African
cargo across the Atlantic!

The bodies of Africans were branded with hot metals,
Their feet and wrists were shackled for bondage,
To keep them in line, Africans were hauled in chains.
Their human dignity was not a question to the civilized
Conscience!

It was called the Triangular Trade System,
From Europe to Africa to the Americas.
It was called the Transatlantic Slave Trade.
On the Atlantic Ocean from Africa to the Americas through
the
dreadful Middle Passage,

Packed in ships from top to bottom,
Like sardines in a can, Africans craved fresh air.
Through pain and hunger, they died in the dungeon,
And to the shirks, the Europeans threw the dead to feast.

To the Indies and Britain, their cargo was taken,
In the streets of Paris and Belgium, a spectacle they were.
But in America, the vilest form of human slavery
John Wesley said he saw firsthand.

George Walters-Sleyon

Africans on the Auction Block in Europe

With the arrival of the ships, the human auction began.
On the slave market, Africans were bought and sold.
The trading was public, with the human goods advertised.
The auction was private, with red ribbons on the doors.

Like things, Europeans sold their African slaves off.
For their plantations, they were auctioned for all to purchase.
Like cows and horses, they reduced Africans to cattle.
For pleasure, Europeans scrambled for a Buck or a Wench.

Pieces of cotton they picked for their superiors' comfort,
For rum and sugar, they were worked to death.
Cities they built like Liverpool, Bristol, London, DC, Paris…
For the slave had no right that the Whiteman must recognize.

African dignity Europeans painfully sought to distort.
Their African dignity Europeans spit upon.
Their human dignity Europeans destroyed for gain.
This human cruelty Europeans could not abandon.

As goods of pray, Africans were their means of wealth.
The economic gains were worth the cruelty.
To trade in humans, their hearts were cold.
The Africans they saw as economic units.

George Walters-Sleyon

It is an oxymoron the conscience cannot bear,
That civilization will dabble in this abuse of humanity!
It is an oxymoron the conscience cannot bear.

The Heterosexual Slave Master

Sex and rape the slave masters used to intimidate,
Sex and rape the slave masters used to discipline,
Sex and rape the slave masters used to control,
Sex and rape the slave masters used as pleasure.

It was an absolute authority that the slave master was given.
Ask John Locke in the *Fundamental Constitutions.*
Anger and arrogance, the slave, must not display!
Wiping and raping were the master's price.

The master ran a harem of slave women.
The appealing slave girl was the masters' price.
For Thomas Jefferson, it was his right to rape Sally Hemings
and to birth six children for him.
Who dares to tell the master it was wrong to rape his slaves?

The notion of slave marriage was unthinkable.
The master owned the slaves, their sexuality, their labor
With absolute power, the master was the "husband."
With absolute power, he could rape, sell, or kill his slave.

We must not forget the practice of slave breeding.
Congress ended the transatlantic slave trade in 1807,
But the Act left the domestic slave trade untouched.
This Congressional Act led to slave breeding farms for
the domestic slave markets.

The Bucks were used as stallions as the master demanded
The Wenches were caged to produce babies.
The babies were made for the and the slave market
He sold the babies when they were of age while the mothers
were left in bleeding trauma.

George Walters-Sleyon

The Homosexual Slave Master

Then there is the case of the homosexual slave master,
Not often talked about but indeed existed.
The slave master could publicly buck-break the arrogant
Buck.
With the practice of buck-breaking, the master was in control.

Like the raping of the Wench, the Buck was subdued.
In public, the macho Buck was publicly humiliated.
Like the raping of the wench, the Buck was humbled.
In the breaking of the Buck, racial and sexual
dominance, the master perfected.

With impunity, the master could beat his slave to death.
With impunity, the master could starve his slave to death.
With impunity, the master could prostitute his slave to death.
To death, the slave was destined at the wimp of the master.

Sex and rape the slave masters used to intimidate
Sex and rape the slave masters used to discipline
Sex and rape the slave masters used to control
Sex and rape the slave masters used as pleasure.

George Walters-Sleyon

Abolition in Britain and America

In 1833, the British ended the trade in human beings,
Wilberforce was an instrument with a Divine mandate.
In Amazing Grace, John Newton regrets,
He was a human trader and had sinned against God and
Africans.

The human trade and economic industry,
Understood by Locke and Ashford, and Tilton,
An economical means to generational prosperity,
Yet, in Wesley's advice, Wilberforce was victorious.

The trade in human beings ended in Britain,
But Americans demanded a civil war.
Abraham Lincoln could bear the guilt no more,
Yet, in the Thirteenth Amendment, slavery is preserved.

32 years later, the North and the South to war they went,
To end the human trade in 1865.
A military battle they ardently fought,
The desire for slave labor the United States could not shake off

Though slavery was moribund by the law,
Ipso facto, every Whiteman was a law enforcement officer Du
Bois explains.
Mob and vigilante justice in law enforcement were birth.
They used the Black Codes and Convict Leasing System to
recoup lost Black labor.

George Walters-Sleyon

Lynching!

The end of slavery marked the birth of the era of terror.
Jim Crow laws were passed to repossess Black bodies.
The end of slavery marked the birth of legal suppression,
Pig Laws were passed to repossess Black humanity.

After Emancipation, White nationalism became the norm.
In 1865 the KKK was born with White supremacist ideologies.
To keep Blacks in "their place," White nationalists advanced.
While the target of the KKK is the disdain for Black humanity

Under Jim Crow laws, Blacks' flesh was on display,
The burning of Black bodies was spectacular to White folks.
Church services were scorned to jubilate over Black lynching,
And images of Black lynching became sought-after souvenirs.

Ida B. Wells could not stomach this wickedness of the heart.
Off to Europe, she fled to tell the world that Americans were
masturbating on lynching Black bodies.
Lynching was Black horror porn in living colors for White
folks

But to Billie Holiday, lynching depicted the "Strange Fruits" of
burning Black flesh in the heart of America.

Lynching, the White mobs knew as the ultimate weapon.
Blacks were in constant terror of this post-slavery terrorism,
They came from Church to lynch Black bodies and souls.
Black children and Black women were no exception,
Emmett Till can tell you more.

Enough of Black flesh White bigots have not had.
From Jim Crow to police brutality: the legal lynching of Blacks
abounds.
Ask Eric Garner, George Floyd, Breona Taylor, etc.
For James Cone, Black lynching depicts the re-crucifixion of
Jesus Christ.

George Walters-Sleyon

It is an oxymoron the conscience cannot bear,
That democracy will dabble in this abuse of humanity!
It is an oxymoron the conscience cannot bear.

Their Penal Subjugation

The end of slavery was the beginning of incarceration,
They designed Jim Crow laws to re-enslave free blacks.
, Blacks were convicted and leased to companies for the crime
of vagrancy
It was slavery as punishment, the 13th Amendment declares.

Cheap labor through human bondage continues.
Du Bois in Atlanta laments the chain gang,
The quest to dehumanize, regardless of human anguish,
The police system Du Bois exclaimed, was inherently racist.

Africans bundled in chains from their homeland,
Africans handcuffed in pain behind bars,
Africans sardined to labor in the West,
Africans handicapped as citizens in the U.S. behind bars.

They claim Blacks for crimes are the cream of the crop,
Du Bois did lament the "color of crime" in the United States,
It is a lie, he argues, to ease the conscience,
But Blacks in U.S. suburbs are in prison pits.

The profit margin is the prison's goal.
Economic gain synonymous with the slave trade it is.
True justice and rehabilitation are the forsaken goals,
While a multitude perishes in prisons as economic
units in the United States Penal System.

The criminalization of the Black man is the utmost claim.
While the rapists, drug users, and serial killers we know.
Yet, the Black man, the criminal we continue to claim,
An oxymoron that pricks the conscience.

George Walters-Sleyon

They Have Sinned Against God and the Africans

They have sinned against God and the people of Africa!
The Arab slave traders have sinned!
The Muslim slave traders have sinned!
The Catholic Popes: Nicholas V and Alexander V1 have
sinned.

The Muslim traders stole African gold and African labor,
While Arabization and Islamification were their covering.
The Catholic papal bulls of 1452, 1455, and1493 were racial,
Africans, they claimed, were beneath their Catholic
Eurocentrism.

They have sinned! Repentance, Reparation they must offer!
They have sinned! Britain, Belgium, Holland, United States.
They have sinned! Portugal, France, Spain, Scotland,
They have sinned! Locke, Hume, Kant, Hegel, Jefferson,
Thomas Leyland, Sir. James Stirling Richard Oswald …

150 Ramadans for Muslims and Arabs with prayers,
The Islamic prayers of *Fajr, Dhuhr, Asr, Maghrib,* and *Isha'a*
For the Catholics, 150 *Our Fathers, Hail Mary*s, and Rosaries.
They have sinned against God and the people of Africa.

For Britain, Belgium, Holland, and the United States,
For Portugal, France, Spain, Scotland, and Denmark,
Reparation and Repentance for their bloody wealth,
They have sinned against God and the people of Africa.

Repentance, Apologies, and Reparation:
For Africans thrown overboard during the Middle Passage
For Africans raped, murdered, babies bred and sold as slaves
willy-nilly.
For Africans who built London, Liverpool, Bristol, the
American
South, Washington D.C, Paris, Oxford and Cambridge
Universities, Harvard, Yale, Princeton, Columbia
Universities, etc.

George Walters-Sleyon

It is an oxymoron the conscience cannot bear
That civilization will dabble in this abuse of humanity
It is an oxymoron the conscience cannot bear

The World

The world is a large stage. It is a stage of perceptions and consciousness duly designed, defined, and delightful. Nevertheless, it is a stage of apathy and apartheid, always needing a cycle of construction and de-construction.

The Ridiculous is Anointed!

Will the remains of this abide?
This trampling of sacred cords,
This trashing of secrets attained,
That humanity is not conventional,

To abandon humanity, it demands,
To banish humanity, it condones,
To besiege humanity, it declares,
To abuse humanity it construes.

That humanity is not conventional; they ignore,
To be human, they must not be,
Not to be human, they must depart,
In such departure, affliction is condoned,
While the ridiculous is anointed.

The unconventional has turned conventional,
The reduction to taste acquired,
The demotion to testaments convened,
The confinement of targets accused.

This stripping of humanity is envisioned,
This bleeding of humanity is partitioned,
In sessions past with overt themes, it remains,
In sessions present with covert themes, it retains.

Wealth and privilege the defining mark,
Religion and nationality the destructive marks,
Tribes and tribalism a defining mark,
Race and racism the deafening marks,
And the ridiculous is anointed.

George Walters-Sleyon

The Ridiculous is Uncrucified!

The poor in anguish remains,
In poverty, they sail in misery,
Sold in bondage to angst assailing,
The poor in anxiety bears the assault,
The assaults of generational abuses.

Imprisoned to enrich the wealthy,
Through prison camps, their wealth define,
Their worth and wealth prisoners define,
The poor in prison humanity imprisoned.

The refusal to see dishonesty heightens,
The refusal to hear denial reasoned,
The refusal to know falsehood enlightened,
The refusal to feel denial ripens,
While the ridiculous is uncrucified.

What is ridiculous is not sacrilegious,
The abuse of humanity is not anathema,
Wealth they acquire through human abuse.
What is ridiculous is uncrucified

Before our eyes, humanity collapse,
Before our eyes, humanity is sacrificed,
Before our eyes, humanity in despair unfolds,
With this, we watch the crowning of the ridiculous.

The profit abounds with this human desecration,
Human commodity abounds with generational profits,

While bleeding abounds with abject poverty,
The absurd is sacralized for profiteering
While the ridiculous remains uncrucified.

George Walters-Sleyon

The Sacred is Anathematized!

The walls have fallen,
The bridges are falling,
The profane is enthroned,
The profound is dethroned,
The strings are failing.

The disharmony of ancient chords,
The trampling on sacred chords,
Indiscipline is exalted,
Discipline is exiled,
While the sacred is maligned.

The sacred is made malignant,
The secret is conflicted,
Sacrifice is refused,
The sacrament scandalized,
What is sacrilegious is made sacrosanct.

We have arrived at our ancient claims,
We have anointed our ancient claims,
Our claims a mere illusion in manifest glory,
Our claims a mere delusion in manifest glory,
Yes, the excellence of manifest glory the world together
excludes.

The Sacred is Anathematized!

George Walters-Sleyon

The Heart is Cold!

When empathy is trampled upon,
And apathy is prevailed upon,
The coldness of the heart is exalted thereon.

When society is lonely,
Its people are lonely,
Society is cold when the heart is cold.

The fear of the other is the test of its society,
The prejudice of its laws is the test of its leader,
The isolation of its member is the test of its communities.

The flight of empathy is the flight of sympathy,
The flood of apathy is the flow of apartheid,
The heart is cold when souls are atrophy.

George Walters-Sleyon

The Confidence of the Soul

The poems in this category are instructional. They are designed to provide practical knowledge and practical insights into the affairs of this life.

Can a Man Declare Himself Innocent?

With the wings of his thoughts, he thinks of a thing,
With the stirring of his thoughts, he discerns a thing,
With the wings of his thoughts, he flees to a thing,
With the flight of his thoughts, he plans a thing.

When with the plans of his thoughts, he creates a thing,
When with the plans of his thoughts, he crafts a thing,
When with the crafting of his thoughts, he births a thing,
We behold the manifestation in awe or disgust.

The ears only hear what is said,
The eyes only see what is birthed,
The hands only touch what is made,
The heart only feels what it senses.

The eyes judge what it sees,
The ears judge what is heard,
The hands judge what is touched,
The heart judges what it feels,
Can a man declare himself innocent?

George Walters-Sleyon

The Pursuit of Ideas

Education is empowerment to the disempowered,
The disempowered is empowered through education.

The senses nurture the ideas of the foolish,
The intellect nurtures the ideas of the wise,
Despise the pursuit of ideas and be despised,
Crave the pursuit of ideas and be pursued.

Pursue education and empower your soul,
Despise education and disempower your soul.

A man of strength gathers wealth,
But a man of education may steal his wealth,
For strength is nurtured by food,
And education is nourished by ideas.

A poor man gathers wealth,
But another man eye's him.

Envy the wealth of the wealthy and be worthless,
Crave the wits of the wealthy and be worthy,
Envy the poverty of the poor and be poor,
Crave the peace of the poor and be prosperous.

He who is insecure is disempowered,
He who is secure is empowered,

Ideas are discerned,
Ideas are developed,
Ideas are derived,
Because good ideas are divine.

George Walters-Sleyon

The Threesome of Knowing

Knowledge is a fact,
Understanding is insight,
Wisdom is divine.

Knowledge is concrete,
Understanding is conception,
Wisdom is conceived.

George Walters-Sleyon

The Trouble of the Insecure

I see a man who resorts to the use of his strength,
His empowerment is his strength,
For brute strength is his security.

I saw a man who resorted to his tribe,
His tribe was his empowerment,
For brute tribalism was his strength.

I see a man who resorts to his opinions,
His opinion is his empowerment,
But brute fanaticism is his strength.

I saw a man who resorted to his race,
His race was his empowerment,
And brute racism was his strength.

One man despises another man and seeks his destruction,
Another man despises him and flees from him,
The One who seeks his destruction and the One who flees are
both insecure.

George Walters-Sleyon

I Dwell in the Permanent

I dwell in the permanent,
For the preeminent is within,
To dwell in the permissive.

Is to dwindle in perplexity,
Therefore, I gasp at profundity,
And wither the paralysis.

George Walters-Sleyon

The Introspective

Cleansing

The poems in this category are introspective. They speak to the process of looking within as the goal of self-analysis and self-discovery.

The Process

In the crucible of the furnace is pruning,
In the crucifixion of the flesh is preparation,
In the crowning of the flame is prosperity.

George Walters-Sleyon

Turn Upon Yourself and Be Found!

Turn upon yourself and be fine,
Turn upon yourself and be refined,
Turn upon yourself and be defined,
Turn upon yourself and be found.

The you that is fine is the you refined,
The you that is refined is the you defined,
Since the you defined is the you affirmed,
Turn upon yourself and be found

George Walters-Sleyon

Limitation

The Limitation of soap: it washes what is seen.
The Limitation of salt: it seasons what it touches.
The Limitation of the wind: it blows away what is seen.
The Limitation of the Spirit: it is deemed by the will.
The Limitation of the will it is a limitation unto the self.

George Walters-Sleyon

Beauty and Wisdom

It is said about the beautiful,
Your face is easy on the eyes,
It is said about the handsome,
Your face is soft on the eyes.

But it is said of Wisdom,
You eliminate the hardness of the face,
And it is said of the wise,
Your face is soft on the ignorant.

George Walters-Sleyon

Above and Below in Contrast

Purified from above,
Purified from below,
Sanctified from above,
Sanctified from below.

What is from above is imputed,
What is from below is imported,
What is from below is directed,
What is from above is designated.

Above is the mainstream departed,
Below is the mainstream displayed,
Below abides in the shadow of composition,
Above abides in the shadows of simplicity.

Deny me not the attainment from above,
Deliver me from the attention from below,
Depend I stand on the strength of above,
Desire I display in strength below.

George Walters-Sleyon

My Ten Principles of Life

I.   Pray since you do not know.

II.   Be silent and studious since multiple sounds surround you.

III.   Speak and be heard, for your calling is real.

IV.   Seek progress through diligence since lack of progress seeks digression.

V.   Pay your debt and be free of anxiety since debt and stress are the twins of pain.

VI.   Pursue religion and learn virtue – despise religion and learn vice.

VII.   Be disciplined and learn devotion – despise discipline and be destroyed.

VIII.   Respect others and be respected – despise others and be despised.

IX.   Respect your elders and be blessed – reproach your elders and be cursed.

X.   Pursue pleasure with discernment – reject discernment and be derailed.

George Walters-Sleyon

Reflective Serenade

These are a series of poems concerning the understanding of self-introspection. Gazing within to know oneself as an instructional approach to self-discovery.

The Piercing of Light

Light pierces
And darkness is displayed.

Light pierces
And delusion is displaced.

Light pierces
And death is delayed.

The piercing of light enlightens the consciousness.
The piercing of light lightens the conscience.
The piercing of light enlightens the conscious One.

George Walters-Sleyon

I am Instructed

Awakened in the night as a sleeping student,
Awakened from a night of sleeping stupor,
I am instructed,
I am not instructed.

Like the gentle breeze of the Ocean,
And the gentle breath of the Orient,
I hear a voice,
It is the inclination of a superior voice.

I am instructed in the hidden place,
I am instructed in the inner place,
A place attained,
A place within.

Like the majestic sight of the Rising Sun,
And the majestic scene of the Resting Sun,
I hear a voice,
Voice so subtle and yet so sublime.

I am awakened to reflect,
I am awakened to deflect,
Reflect on the voice instructing breath,
Deflect from voice instructing death.

Like the conscious guardian imparting claims,
Like the conscious guardian impacting claims,

I am instructed,
I am not instructed.

George Walters-Sleyon

Light Hidden in Darkness

Not the darkness of external lightness,
Nor lightness of exterior darkness,
The petulance of lightness is defined,
The petulance of darkness discerned.

The birth of light, darkness defines,
The birth of darkness, light discerns,
Refrain from the darkness the eyes perceive,
Refrain from the lightness the eyes perceive.

Turn away from the apparent sight,
Turning away from the oblivious sight,
The obvious is reality discerned,
The oblivious is reality distorted.

I search the path of this true light,
Hidden in the crevice of darkness,
It's grasping I desire,
It's a glimpse I must pursue.

The eyes of eyes behold it,
Sight betrays it,
Reason distorts it,
Intellect betrays it.

Its path one must tread,
Its pain one must bear,
In its pace, one is led,
Since in its peace, one is made better,

George Walters-Sleyon

The Movement

Progress outward by
    turning inward.

Progress inward by
    turning outward.

Proceed towards by
    turning within.

Proceed within by
    turning toward.

Progress internally by
    turning externally.

George Walters-Sleyon

Know This

Do not lose your hope, for the hopeless is harpless.
Do not lose your dream, for the dreamless is doomed.
The hopeless are harpless and cannot sing,
The dreamless is doomed and cannot survive.

Study the path of the fearful
For locked in their heart is uncertainty.
Study the path of the impertinent
For locked in their heart is insolence.

Study the path of the boisterous
Locked in their heart is revenge.
Study the path of the cynic
For locked in their heart is fear.

Pick up the cards and pack them.
Pick up the scattered corn and plant them.
For as the As reside in the scattered cards
So, your gold resides in the planted corn.

George Walters-Sleyon

The Struggle of the Soul

This struggle of the soul within
Is the strangling of the soul without.
This longing of the soul to be "There"
Is the loneliness of the soul not "There."

The soul in constant tension
The battle for deliverance from strains.
The strains of this embodiment
Is the flight to disembodiment.

It is the desire to be
But the desertion to not be.
The "is" of the conflict to be
The "is" of the desire to be.

The rising of the soul
The raising of the self.
The flight from strains
The flight from constraints.

Rankling abides for a while
Up the hill, this rankling subsides.
Over this rankling, the soul prevails
The soul this rankling enkindles.

Instruct me not in the burden of the soul!
Teach me not the burden of the soul.
This burden my soul has known.
In this struggle, my soul is known.

George Walters-Sleyon

He Sits in Solitude

He sits in solitude
In solitude, he sits.
He sits to reflect
To reflect, he sits.

Sitting in solitude, he reflects
Reflecting in solitude, he deflects.
In deflecting, he is aware
In awareness, reflecting is perfected.

Perfection in deflecting a reflection of the conflict,
Conflict in deflecting a reflection of affliction.
Affliction in reflecting travailing toward perfection
To grasp the reflected is to attain the reflected.

The agitation of the soul is the quest to attain.
The progress of the intellect is the quest to retain.
The affliction of the soul is to remain what it attains.
The perversion of the intellect is to retain what it deflects.

He sits in solitude
In solitude, he sits.
He sits to reflect
To reflect, he sits.

The circle he repeats
The repeating he deflects.
The deflection he rejects
Till the reflected he projects.

George Walters-Sleyon

Drop the Gun!

Drop the Gun
Pick up the Book.
The gun will kill you
The Book will fill you.

George Walters-Sleyon

Nature and Notions

The birds sing,
The flowers bloom,
Life goes on.

The river flows,
The sea rolls,
Life moves on.

The chill of the air,
The cold of the day,
Living continues.

Birth takes place,
Death takes place,
Life emerges.

Decisions are made,
Policies are made,
Lives are affected.

Thoughts prevail,
Thinking prevails,
The living reflects.

Proposals are made,
Plans are constructed,
Your life is defined.

George Walters-Sleyon

Allow

Allow a person to rebuke you.
Allow them to rebuke you in public.
Allow a public rebuke to chastise you.

Allow chastisement to mend you.
Allow this Amendment to prepare you.
Allow those who rebuke you to glory in your chastisement,

Since it is for the glory that they rebuke you.

George Walters-Sleyon

Learn the Ways of the Gentle Breeze

Follow the path of intuition,
Follow the path of the Divine,
With these, the colors of life begin to bloom.

Despise not the inclusions of your heart,
Despise not the exclusions of your heart,
With these tensions, the heart is stable.

Listen to the inklings that speak from afar,
Listen to the inklings that speak to defer,
Learn the movement of the unseen eyes.

The past enfolded in the present discern,
The present enfolded in the future descends,
Learn the ways of the Gentle Breeze.

Resist the noise that clouds the sound,
Respond to the noise that cleans the sound,
In noise and harmony, the soul is sound.

Take your cue from the voice that leads,
Take your cue from the voice you hear,
The voice in silence speaks with volume.

On to the height of the gentle ladder,
Climb the ladder step by step,
It ends in solace and a blissful stir.

Descend from the height of the gentle ladder,
Into the abyss of human experience,
It is the context of not mere repose.

George Walters-Sleyon

Don't Be a Fool!

The bar was set,
The standards exulted,
The rules established,
The precepts settled.

Hunger may strike,
Thirst may abound,
Need in abundance,
But your future, you do not trade.

He comes from afar,
To defile your shrine.
His perception of life,
You must analyze

Refuse the bait,
Reject the snare,
Renounce the trap,
Reclaim your dignity.

The theories are framed,
The Perceptions are defined,
The laws are fostered,
Their doom is executed.

Don't sign the paper,
Your heritage you trade.

The enticement of money,
the ensnaring of your soul.

A fool you are
To batter your pride.
His heritage he protects,
While your heritage he profanes.

George Walters-Sleyon

Language Reflects my Limitation

I express my thoughts with language,
I explain my thoughts in language,
I expound my thoughts through language.

With language, my thoughts, I define,
With language, my thoughts, I defend,
With language, my thoughts, I find.

Thoughts prescribed in prepositions are limited.
Thoughts processed in prepositions are laminated.
Thoughts positioned in prepositions are lamented.

Language proclaims my thoughts in the material.
Language prolongs my thoughts on the material.
Language profanes my thoughts in the material.

Essence defies prepositions,
Essence escapes prepositions,
Essence eludes prepositions.

My thoughts in language I proclaim.
My thoughts in language I profane.
My thoughts in language are profound.

Being rejects prepositions,
Spirit negates prepositions,
Being renounces prepositions.

Language reflects materialism,
Prepositions reflect mortality,
Essence reflects immortality.

George Walters-Sleyon

I am Down to My Last

I am down to my last
But I am not the rest.
Can't give up on this test
I must be the best.

I heard the word believe,
Doubt and unbelieve are not priceless.
To believe is to have a belief,
But doubt may steal your prize from you.

Drawn to my last, I am not bound.
The conflicting traces of despair resound.
I am confident my upward courage will abound,
Since the prevailing peace of Providence is my bond.

When down to my last, I stand.
The emergence of peace in pain arises,
No clue I've got to the source of this witness,
But simply to believe its soothing traces.

I will not fear the stings of despair!
Its dart of piercing arrows shall be destroyed.
In the immutable, I have discerned,
Not to trust the darts of despair.

George Walters-Sleyon

My Search for a Platform

My search is for a platform to perform.
Platforms are created; they are not given,
Platforms are given; they are not created,
But be aware when your platform arrives.

I am informed that platforms are opportunities.
Platforms come, and platforms go,
Learn the art of knowing your platform.
Learn the art of owning your platform.

Platforms are gifts; they must be cherished.
To perform on a platform is to excel in your ability.
Platforms are gifts with diverse appearances,
To perform on a platform is to excel in your capability.

Your platform shall come, I often hear,
A platform is prepared for the message you have.
Your platform shall appear. Look around you,
A platform is primed. Don't let it disappear.

George Walters-Sleyon

Meditations

These poems are the contemplative expressions of human angsts. They are prayers, supplications, and Divine assurances depicting human's quests for intervention beyond their capabilities.

Prayers I Will Offer!

Prayers I Will Offer
To the hearing ear, I whisper,
At night in absolute oblation,
My contrition I employ,
To be heard in deep anxiety.

In prayers, I supplicate,
To the listening ear, I plea.
My voice I lift at the breaking of dawn.
From his burden, I seek relief,
In prayers, my supplications I present.

With prayers, I entreat,
The watchful eyes of the shepherd's gaze,
My condition to God is well known.
Yet to entreat, I am required to do,
To display my trust on unchanging grounds.

In prayers, I watch,
Longing for God's arrival,
In the cool of the day, in the shadows of the blistering Sun
My soul in the watchful pose it is stationed,
To await the arrival of God.

With prayers, I praise,
In gratitude for solemn relief,

In gratitude for the sudden reply,
My soul unburdened; my soul redeemed.
There I cherish the sweet reprieve.

George Walters-Sleyon

Help Me!

Help me,
And I shall be helped.

Deliver me,
And I shall be delivered.

Free me,
And I shall be free.

I carry a yoke,
That only you can unyoke.

I carry a burden,
That only you can unburden.

Help Me,
And I shall be helped.

George Walters-Sleyon

This Twoness of Me

The twoness of life,
Living in spirituality,
Living in secularity.

The twoness of consciousness,
Awareness of the sacred,
Awareness of the profane.

The twoness of self,
The self on display,
The self in hiding.

What is the betweenness of this twoness,
What is the twinness of this twoness,
It is the absolute coming together into Oneness.

George Walters-Sleyon

O Lord Our Teacher!

Oh Lord, our teacher,
It is you who teaches,
And we are taught.
Grant that we may follow your teachings.

It is you who instructs,
And we are instructed.
It is you who enlightens,
And we are enlightened.

Teach us that we may be taught.
Instruct us that we may be instructed.
Enlighten us that we may be enlightened,
For thy fountain of knowledge is endless to our finite faculty.

O Lord Our Teacher!

George Walters-Sleyon

Where is God?

Where is God?
Look within, for God is present!
Look within, for there the Divine abides.

Within is the place of speaking
Without is the place of hearing.
Contrasting sounds construe hearing
Constructing sounds construes speaking

Where is God?
Look within, for God is present!
Look within, for there the Divine abides.

Permeating the cuticles of death,
One hears the Words of the Logos within.
Shattering the conflicting sounds of the exterior,
To bring unto me the interior sounds of inspiring Words.

Where is God?
Look within, for God is present!
Look within, for there the Divine abides.

George Walters-Sleyon

Take Your Issues to the Lord in Prayer

I have issues that I struggle with.
Overwhelming, they are my human issues,
Issues I have acquired along the way.

The implications of my issues I sometimes dread,
They are issues that won't go away,
Yet they are issues I take to the Lord.

On the altar of prayer, these issues I submit.
My issues I present earnestly to God,
Unto God, I declare my imperfections.

In the name of Jesus Christ, I declare my faith.
The search for freedom I request in prayers,
Deliverance from my issues, the Lord is aware.

Take your issues to the Lord, I hear,
He hears the silent cries of human issues.
The quiet tears He always dries.

The feeble knees He always strengthens,
Your issues Jesus Christ will resolve.
Take your issues to the Lord in prayer.

My issues at the altar, I therefore offer.
With God's intervention, I relinquish my issues.
On the altar, I deposit my human issues.

Issues I relinquish on the divine altar
Although I am conscious of their return to God, I trust to keep
them safe.
In the Lord, my issues are dealt with.

Take your Issues to the Lord in Prayer.

George Walters-Sleyon

The Lord is My Shadow!

The Lord is my shadow!
I need not fear.
Beset by grief,
His peace surrounds me.

In a cloudy storm,
I need not flee.
The Lord He is there,
His presence surrounds me.

In the night of the gloom,
I need not fret.
Broken by sorrow,
His power surrounds me.

The Lord is my shadow,
I need not faint.
In search of favor,
His provision surrounds me.

George Walters-Sleyon

What Do I Long For?

What do I long for?
I know not.
What do I desire?
I acknowledge less.

My passion is wrapped in your desire.
Indeed, I know not what I desire.
Since to know is to come to the fullness of knowledge,
Such knowledge I have not attained.

Such knowledge I struggle to retain,
It is knowledge of true knowledge.
It is knowledge of true acknowledgment.
Toward this knowledge, I am only driven.

Towards this knowledge, I am drawn.
A spark of this knowledge I encounter,
A spark of this knowledge I embrace,
Its fullness always eludes me.

A constant striving, I endure,
A constant evasion I endure.
A constant pursuit I engage,
Yet it is you I desire.

You, my eyes perceive not,
You, my eyes, receive not.
In the darkening of the world, you are beheld,
In the lightening of the world, we behold you.

Yet this shifting within is confounding,
This shaking in my abode confuses me.
At a cross-road, I am made to stand,
Longing for certainty in what I long for.

George Walters-Sleyon

God Has Not Brought Me This Far

God has not brought me this far to leave me!
The tides may increase,
The waves may rumble,
But I am not alone.

He has not brought me this far to depart from me!
Of this certainty, I am aware.
Thoroughly convinced that there is an end to my anxiety,
He walks with me.

God has not brought me this far to abandon me!
These words I have heard.
Springing forth from within,
Unrehearsed to console me.

He has not brought me this far to renounce me!
Strengths I have gathered from the distance,
Courage I have gathered for the distance,
To face the distance, I am assigned.

God has not brought me this far to forsake me!
This I know, and I have come to cherish.
This knowledge is specific, and it comes from within,
That God is in control, a reality I cherish.

George Walters-Sleyon

When Your Niche Arrives!

Traverse the great waters,
Traverse the great weather,
Your niche awaits its timely arrival.
Spin in formal circles,
Spin with informal cycles,
Your niche is a solemn place for self-expression.

It seems your niche is a moment proposed,
It seems your niche a momentum prepared,
Isn't the niche a transcendent design?
You, the target this niche pursues,
You, the object of this niche pursuit,
Isn't it you this niche elect?

With eyes on you, your niche is waiting,
To unfold to you with absolute delight,
Yet your movements this niche upholds.
But not for long will this niche select,
Unfazed by the unparalleled rhythm of your life,
Niches direct their elected targets.

At you, your niche continues to gaze,
With solemn gaze, it awaits your listening eyes,
Conditioned by time your niche is coming.
In the un-distant distance, your niche unfolds,

Its arrival in time you will undoubtedly know
Your niche is here. Do you know it has arrived?

George Walters-Sleyon

The Burden of Bended Knees

I fall on my knees in the morning to pray,
The burden, this time too heavy to carry.
Help I really need at this time,
To lift this burden from me in time.

This burden, I know, is not my lot,
Its nature, I understand, is for a while.
A human experience this burden is,
A divine experience prepared for me.

My knees though weary in constant contrition,
My silent petition, I pause to whisper.
He knows my falling as well as my failing,
To Him, I owe my constant pace.

Arise, I hear from your bended knees,
Too weary of bearing your spirit's needs.
In prayers, your answer comes in speed,
To satisfy your weary plea.

Oh, forsake me not while this burden I bear,
A shame I am sometimes, I know.
With guilt assailing my honest quest,
My Redeemer, I know my yoke He breaks.

He directs my path to bring me peace,
Though I know not when He starts His divine intervention.

The end I see is fully pleasing,
To keep me close to this resting place.

In rebellion, I forever cannot abide,
To suspect the material, the immaterial, I pursue.
His guidance I relish as I walk this path,
To abide in His presence, a promise assured.

Come unto me, my weary One,
Stay where I place you till the time is ripe.
Your burden I ease till the time is right,
I am your peace, your Jehovah Sharon.

George Walters-Sleyon

It is Not Late

It is not late, I often hear!
Your time is coming to have your share,
I have prepared your share in this life,
Though its coming may tarry a while.

It is not late; I am reminded!
Others I see with constant progress,
Their progress I wish I had as well,
Yet, I am often reminded that my progress is coming.

Do not be moved by what you see,
Your heart may ache with failing wants.
I prepare your desire to bring you peace,
To satisfy your needs in finite time.

A spacious place I am preparing for you,
Age and time cannot delay.
I move the hand of the silent clock,
To bring to pass my plans prepared.

It is not late again, I counsel,
Your destiny I fashion only for you.
Your path in life is designed for you,
To accomplish in you my desired goal.

I am your solace in the sliding path,
Your lane in silence I seek to protect.

I am your friend who knows your fears,
Your healer unseen to make you whole.

It is not late; your time is coming,
All will see and know it is time.
You, I have kept for the time I planned,
You are mine, and I know your needs!

I have counseled you, so hear it well!
You have heard it and often said,
It is my word to you, I repeat.
It is not late. Your time is now!

George Walters-Sleyon

Made in the USA
Columbia, SC
22 December 2022

ff2e5f42-f603-4ad9-86b2-35e83ebcb965R02